What Beautiful Birds!

Consider This

A **declarative sentence** makes a statement and ends with a period.

An **interrogative sentence** asks a question and ends with a question mark.

An **imperative sentence** states a command or gives an order and ends with a period.

An **exclamatory sentence** expresses strong feeling and ends with an exclamation point.

Read each sentence. Notice that the end punctuation has been omitted. Choose the word that describes the sentence.

1 People in the United States are familiar with the robin
    G declarative   E interrogative   F imperative   D exclamatory

2 Is it true that some robins stay north throughout the winter
    A declarative   I interrogative   C imperative   J exclamatory

3 Always keep a lookout for robins
    E declarative   D interrogative   L imperative   A exclamatory

4 A bright spring morning is a good time to see a robin
    H declarative   B interrogative   J imperative   G exclamatory

5 What beautiful flute-like music they make
    I declarative   K interrogative   B imperative   F exclamatory

6 Could that be a robin singing
    F declarative   J interrogative   H imperative   L exclamatory

7 The robin can often be seen tugging on a worm
    B declarative   F interrogative   I imperative   C exclamatory

8 Do you know what kind of berries they eat
    L declarative   C interrogative   G imperative   B exclamatory

9 A robin's nest is usually made of mud, twigs, and straw
    K declarative   G interrogative   E imperative   I exclamatory

10 Look at the sturdy construction
    D declarative   H interrogative   A imperative   K exclamatory

11 How beautiful their blue-green eggs are
    J declarative   L interrogative   K imperative   E exclamatory

12 Count the number of robins that you see each morning
    C declarative   A interrogative   D imperative   H exclamatory

Objective: Identify the four types of sentence structures: declarative, interrogative, imperative, and exclamatory.

1

The Ancient Anasazi

Match each group of words in List 1 to its corresponding subject or predicate in List 2 to form a factual statement about the Anasazi people.

List 1	List 2
1. Interesting pottery	A. They also wove
2. lived in the Southwest.	B. irrigated the land.
3. Many long ditches	C. was made from clay.
4. were used to build houses.	D. Bricks made of mud
5. Only the men	E. The Anasazi people
6. were called "cliff dwellers."	F. These people, who lived in canyons,
7. were all grown on the canyon floor.	G. farmed and hunted.
8. Women in the tribe	H. was hot and dry.
9. strong yucca plant fibers into baskets.	I. Corn, squash, beans, and sunflowers
10. Soap	J. was made from plant roots.
11. The southwest climate	K. The Anasazi's climate and environment
12. preserved artifacts that we can see today.	L. prepared the food.

Objective: Identify the subject part and the predicate part of sentences, using context.

Wonders of China

Consider This

The **complete subject** is all the words that make up the subject of the sentence. The most important word (or words) in the complete subject is called the **simple subject** or the **subject of the verb**.

→[Many different <u>explorers</u>] have discovered new things.

[complete subject] simple subject

Identify the complete subject, then find the simple subject.

Think. Who or what **is** the sentence really talking about?

① In 1271, young Marco Polo set sail for China from his home in Venice, Italy.

② Many years earlier, Marco Polo's father traveled to China.

③ The adventurous travelers in the group sailed a long distance before reaching their destination.

④ Ancient China was a wealthy and prosperous land.

⑤ The wise Kublai Khan ruled the vast empire of China.

⑥ His spectacular palace impressed the Venetian visitors with its many unusual sights.

⑦ Even the walls of the palace were covered with gold and silver.

⑧ The clever Chinese made silk fabric from the cocoons of silkworms.

⑨ Chinese farmers used water power to grind their grain.

⑩ Unusual and unfamiliar spices flavored the exotic foods of China.

⑪ Many Europeans didn't believe what Marco Polo and his crew described when they returned from their journey.

⑫ European traders were happy to find so many wonderful things in China.

Answer Box ·

A	B	C	D	E	F
Europeans	Kublai Kahn	spices	walls	Chinese	traders
G	H	I	J	K	L
travelers	farmers	China	Marco Polo	palace	father

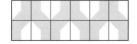

Objective: Identify the complete subject and the simple subject of sentences.

3

Remember the Alamo!

Read the article about the Alamo. Note information that will help you identify the complete and simple predicates in the sentences on the next page.

The Alamo

By 1821, American colonists moving west had settled in parts of Texas that belonged to Mexico. At first, the Mexican government didn't bother the new settlers, but in 1830 Mexico passed a law to stop more settlers from coming to Texas.

In 1834, General Santa Anna took control of the Mexican government and made himself the president. He led soldiers into Texas to enforce Mexican laws and collect taxes from the settlers.

The Texans did not want to pay taxes to Mexico, so they attacked Santa Anna's soldiers on December 5, 1835, in San Antonio. The Mexican soldiers were driven away for a short time, but Santa Anna could not accept this rebellion. Two months later, he returned to San Antonio with 2,000 soldiers and a plan to take back the city.

The Texas rebels secured themselves in the Alamo, an old Spanish mission church in San Antonio. Fewer than 200 Texans fought bravely against the entire Mexican army. William Travis led the Texans. American frontiersman Davy Crockett from Tennessee fought beside him, but Jim Bowie, who was also there, was too sick to fight.

On March 6, 1836, after 13 days of battle, the Alamo was surrounded by the Mexican army and taken. All the men who defended the mission were killed, but the women and children were spared.

While the battle for the Alamo raged, Texas leaders met elsewhere and declared their independence from Mexico. Sam Houston was named commander of their army. In April, Houston's army attacked the Mexicans and captured General and President Santa Anna. Houston offered to let Santa Anna live if Texas was given its independence. Santa Anna agreed to Houston's terms.

Today, Texas is known as the "Lone Star State" because of its red, white, and blue flag with a single white star.

Consider This

The **complete predicate** in a sentence contains all the words that tell what the subject does or what state it is in. The *main verb* (including helping verbs) in the predicate is called the **simple predicate**.

The people of Texas [<u>won</u> their independence.]

↑
simple predicate   [complete predicate]

Find the *complete predicate* that best completes each sentence.

1 Santa Anna ▣.

2 The Texans ▣.

3 Sam Houston ▣.

4 A small group of Texans ▣.

5 On March 6, 1836, the Alamo ▣.

6 Although greatly outnumbered, the Texans ▣.

Find the *simple predicate* that best completes each sentence.

7 Santa Anna's army ▣ William Travis and Davy Crockett, along with the other men.

8 The Mexicans ▣ the women and children in the Alamo.

9 Later that year, the Texans, led by General Sam Houston, ▣ the Mexican forces.

10 Sam Houston and his men ▣ General and President Santa Anna.

11 Mexico ▣ Texas its independence in exchange for Santa Anna's freedom.

12 People ▣ Texas the "Lone Star State."

Answer Box

A	B	C	D	E	F
call	spared	gave	was surrounded by Mexican soldiers	killed	captured

G	H	I	J	K	L
fought bravely	declared their independence from Mexico in 1836	was named commander of the Texas army	attacked	secured themselves in the Alamo	led an army of Mexican soldiers into Texas

Objective: Read for relevant information in a nonfiction, expository article; identify complete and simple predicates, using context.

Dream On. Yes, I Mean You!

Consider This

An **imperative sentence** states a command or gives an order. It ends with a period. In an **imperative sentence**, the subject is always understood to be *you*.

(You understood) Go to sleep.

subject

Read each sentence. Choose *yes* if the sentence is imperative and the subject is *you* (understood) and *no* if it is not.

1. Almost all mammals dream.   F yes   J no

2. Can you remember your dreams?   D yes   B no

3. Put a pencil and pad of paper by your bed.   E yes   A no

4. Tell yourself that you want to remember your dreams.   I yes   C no

5. It is hard to remember your dreams.   L yes   K no

6. Don't forget to set your alarm clock.   A yes   G no

7. Lie in bed with your eyes closed.   C yes   I no

8. Then, sit up and write down your thoughts.   H yes   E no

9. Normally, people dream every night.   J yes   F no

10. You start dreaming after the deepest stage of sleep.   K yes   D no

11. Your eyes dart around as if you were awake.   B yes   L no

12. Please make a diary of your dreams and illustrate it.   G yes   H no

Objective: Identify you (understood) as the subject in imperative sentences; examine sentence structure.

Sand and Water Are Fun!

Consider This

A **compound subject** is two or more simple subjects that share the same predicate. The simple subjects are usually joined by the conjunctions *and* or *or*.

<u>Katie</u> is a good athlete. <u>Scott</u> is a good athlete, too.   **simple subjects**

<u>Katie and Scott</u> are both good athletes.   **compound subject**

Choose the correct verb tense for the compound subject from the words in color.

1 Becky and Cari (**A** watch, **C** watches) the dolphins race through the water.

2 My orange towel and green blanket (**E** cover, **D** covers) our area of the beach.

3 Watch out! Either a pelican or a seagull (**F** fly, **J** flies) overhead.

4 The seashell and the bottle (**B** look, **G** looks) empty floating in the water.

5 Is it the sand or the water that (**H** are, **C** is) warmer?

6 Dave and Dina (**F** run, **K** runs) down to the pier for some ice cream.

7 The seashell and the bottle (**B** is, **H** are) empty.

8 Does Michele or Jodi (**K** eat, **A** eats) hot dogs at the beach?

9 A seagull and a pelican (**I** fly, **E** flies) through the air.

10 Is it Matt or the twins who (**G** look, **F** looks) the most sunburned?

11 A boy and his dog (**D** watch, **J** watches) the other children playing.

12 Clarisse and Tony (**L** have, **I** has) fun at the beach.

> If the subjects are joined by <u>and</u>, the verb is plural. If the subjects are joined by <u>or</u>, the verb agrees with the subject that is closest to it.

Objective: Identify compound subject and correct subject/verb agreement; examine sentence structure.

7

Flips and Flops

Consider This

A **compound predicate** consists of two or more verbs that have the same subject. The verbs are joined by the conjunctions *and* or *or*.

Martha <u>stretched</u> before gymnastics. Martha <u>exercised</u> before gymnastics.

↑ subject ↑ predicate　　　　↑ subject ↑ predicate

Martha <u>stretched and exercised</u> before gymnastics.

↑ subject　　↑ compound predicate

Remember, ask yourself if *two* things are happening to the *same* subject.

Read each sentence. Choose *yes* if the predicate is compound; *no* if it is not.

1. Gymnastics is popular in America and in Europe.

2. Many people practice and enjoy this sport.

3. Soona dances and leaps across the mats.

4. Reuben hangs from the rings and high bars.

5. His skill fascinates and delights the crowd.

6. The beam is narrow and long.

7. Kristina balances carefully and turns on the beam.

8. She dismounts with ease and grace.

9. Tim and Ben swing on the high bar.

10. Phillip races to the vault and concentrates on his flip.

11. The two coaches guide the gymnasts and encourage them.

12. This sport demands hard work and dedication.

A	yes	D	no
B	yes	L	no
E	yes	I	no
G	yes	C	no
K	yes	J	no
H	yes	A	no
I	yes	B	no
F	yes	H	no
C	yes	F	no
J	yes	E	no
L	yes	K	no
D	yes	G	no

Objective: Identify compound predicates, using context; examine sentence structure.

Dogs Are Our Best Friends

Consider This

A **compound sentence** contains two or more simple sentences joined by one of these conjunctions: *and, or, so, nor, yet, for,* or *but.*

Dogs are our friends. They work hard.	**simple sentences**
Dogs are our friends, and they work hard.	**compound sentence**

Decide if each sentence is *simple* or *compound.*

1. Many breeds of dogs are intelligent and hardworking.

2. Dogs make decisions, and they even solve problems on their own.

3. For example, arctic sled dogs pull heavy sleds and run long distances.

4. They need thick coats of fur, or they could get frostbite.

5. The Siberian husky digs a hole in the snow and curls up in it with its tail over its nose for protection from snowstorms.

6. Sheep dogs herd animals and protect them from predators.

7. Many sheep dogs live and work outside in the cold.

8. The German shepherd breed is known for its loyalty, but other breeds also have this admirable trait.

9. Although German shepherds make excellent guide dogs, it is not the only breed used for this job.

10. Many breeds are trained to work alongside the police, but firefighters prefer to have dalmatians ride in their trucks.

11. Guard dogs must be trained well and be obedient, so trainers begin working with them while they are still puppies.

12. Dogs are useful animals and serve many types of functions for humans.

Simple	Compound
H	I
E	J
K	F
A	G
F	H
I	L
B	K
J	D
L	C
D	A
G	E
C	B

Objective: Discriminate between compound sentences and simple sentences; examine sentence structure.

9

Fragments and Run-Ons

Consider This

A **sentence fragment** is not a complete thought although it is often written and punctuated as if it were a sentence. A fragment is only a phrase or a clause.

Fun to make.

A **run-on sentence**, also called a *comma splice*, occurs when two or more independent clauses are joined only by a comma without a coordinating conjunction (*and, but, or, so, for, yet,* or *nor*).

Masks are fun to make, children like to wear them.

Read about masks. Decide if each group of words is a *sentence fragment*, a *run-on sentence*, or a *compound sentence*.

1 Making a mask to disguise yourself.
  J sentence fragment   A run-on sentence   C compound sentence

2 A variety of materials to use.
  A sentence fragment   D run-on sentence   B compound sentence

3 You can make it from paper, use crayons and markers.
  K sentence fragment   F run-on sentence   H compound sentence

4 Paper maché works well to make masks, and paper grocery bags do too.
  C sentence fragment   E run-on sentence   I compound sentence

5 Be creative, but don't make it too scary.
  I sentence fragment   J run-on sentence   L compound sentence

6 Animal masks of elephants with big ears.
  B sentence fragment   K run-on sentence   A compound sentence

7 Use buttons for eyes, try yarn for hair.
  H sentence fragment   C run-on sentence   F compound sentence

8 Ribbon can be used for hair, or you could use string.
  L sentence fragment   I run-on sentence   G compound sentence

9 Wearing masks at plays or at parties.
  E sentence fragment   L run-on sentence   D compound sentence

10 The people of many cultures around the world.
  D sentence fragment   B run-on sentence   J compound sentence

11 The Japanese use masks in their plays, and the masks show emotions.
  F sentence fragment   G run-on sentence   K compound sentence

12 The Egyptians made gold masks, King Tut had a gold mask.
  G sentence fragment   H run-on sentence   E compound sentence

Objective: Discriminate between sentence fragments, run-on
sentences, and compound sentences; examine sentence
structure.

Snowboarding—An Olympic Sport

Clues

□ = person   ○ = place   ☆ = thing   △ = animal   💡 = idea

Complete the story. Find the correct noun to replace each clue.

The 1998 Winter Olympic Games in **1** ○, were very exciting.

They included the debut of a new **2** ☆. Snowboarding was an

awesome addition to the schedule of Olympic **3** ☆.

Though he was only 12 years old, **4** □ hoped that he might compete

in the Olympics one day. He knew that **5** □ from around the world

would try for a **6** ☆ in the Giant Slalom Race for snowboarding.

Would he ever be good enough to represent his **7** ○?

Ross knew he only had four years until the next Winter Olympics. He

wanted to be ready. He practiced with his **8** □ every day. He loved the

9 💡 of the snow-covered mountains. Every now and then, he would

see a camouflaged fox or white snowshoe **10** △ scurrying across

the newly fallen snow as he sped by.

As Ross maneuvered his way down the side of the **11** ☆, he thought

of winning the gold medal just like his Canadian hero, Ross Rebagliata, had.

When Ross focused on his dream, he was filled with **12** 💡.

> A noun **names** a person, place, thing, animal, or idea.

Answer Box

A	B	C	D	E	F
events	mountain	Ross	rabbit	medal	coach

G	H	I	J	K	L
athletes	beauty	country	Nagano, Japan	happiness	sport

More Than One

Choose the correct plural form of each word.

1	church	B churchs	J churches
2	colony	K colonies	D colonys
3	fox	L foxs	H foxes
4	turkey	H turkeies	I turkeys
5	dress	J dresss	B dresses
6	boy	E boies	L boys
7	pilgrim	C pilgrims	F pilgrimes
8	valley	I valleies	E valleys
9	religion	G religions	C religiones
10	family	D families	A familys
11	settler	A settlers	G settleres
12	community	F communities	K communitys

Think about all the different rules you know to help you form the plural. When in doubt, check the spelling in a dictionary.

Wait!

Thank You for visiting Colonial Village!

Objective: Discriminate between correct and incorrect spelling of plural nouns.

Special Plural Noun Endings

Consider This

Rules for Forming Plural Nouns		
Type of Noun	**Add**	**Examples**
ends in *f* preceded by a consonant	change *f* to *v*, then add *-es*	self, selves wolf, wolves
ends in *f* preceded by a vowel	add *-s*	belief, beliefs
ends in *o* preceded by either a consonant or vowel	add *-s*	zero, zeros rodeo, rodeos
ends in *o* preceded by a consonant—exception to above	add *-es*	echo, echoes potato, potatoes
irregular nouns	change spelling	goose, geese
	remains the same	shrimp, shrimp

Look at the singular noun. Then choose the plural with the correct spelling.

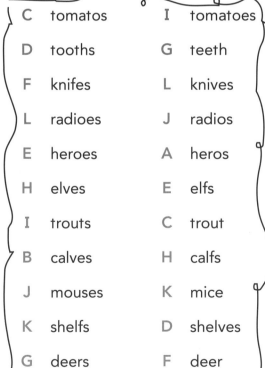

1. tomato   C tomatos   I tomatoes
2. tooth   D tooths   G teeth
3. knife   F knifes   L knives
4. radio   L radioes   J radios
5. hero   E heroes   A heros
6. elf   H elves   E elfs
7. trout   I trouts   C trout
8. calf   B calves   H calfs
9. mouse   J mouses   K mice
10. shelf   K shelfs   D shelves
11. deer   G deers   F deer
12. chief   A chiefs   B chieves

Objective: Discriminate between correct and incorrect spelling of plural nouns.

13

World Travels

Find the noun that matches each puzzle clue.

Across

2 common name for a part of the earth's surface that is raised

4 common name for a big stream of water

7 common name for a very large land mass

10 proper name for a mountain range in Switzerland

11 proper name for one of Earth's very large land masses

12 proper name for the explorer who discovered the Pacific Ocean

Down

1 proper name for a major U.S. river or state

3 proper name for a large body of salt water (2 words)

5 common name for the land where a person is born or is a citizen

6 common name for a very large body of salt water

8 proper name for a nation in Europe

9 common name for a person who discovers new lands and places

Objective: Discriminate between common and proper nouns.

My Kind of Town

Remember, a noun that names something particular, like a person or a country, must be capitalized.

Consider This

Rules for Capitalizing Proper Nouns

Capitalize the names of people and pets.

    Angelo   Fluffy

Capitalize every important word in the names of specific places and things.

    Brookfield Zoo   Statue of Liberty

Capitalize the names of the months, days, and holidays.

    September   Monday   Labor Day

Read about the Cruz family's visit to the city. Choose the number that tells how many nouns in the sentence should be capitalized.

1. The cruz family and their dog, pedro, arrived in chicago, illinois, on friday.

    F 4   C 5   A 6

2. salvador cruz decided that the family would explore the museum of science and industry on saturday morning.

    H 4   J 5   H 6

3. That afternoon, they went to the top of the willis tower, and later they walked along michigan avenue.

    K 4   D 5   B 6

4. emilio, the youngest member of the cruz family, begged for a boat ride on lake michigan.

    D 4   A 5   F 6

5. The colored lights of buckingham fountain in grant park looked spectacular at night.

    E 4   L 5   J 6

6. The fourth of july was the next day, and the family planned a picnic at the lincoln park zoo.

    C 4   G 5   I 6

7. The weather on sunday was cloudy, so alicia and her parents decided to tour the art institute.

    J 4   E 5   K 6

8. A guide, named mr. andrews, showed them paintings by renoir, monet, and picasso.

    I 4   B 5   E 6

9. The spanish painter diego valasquez was their favorite, but they also liked the sculptures by degas.

    L 4   H 5   G 6

10. mrs. cruz said she would like to go to europe and visit france and spain.

    B 4   I 5   C 6

11. When the sun peeked out, the family drove along lake shore drive to navy pier.

    G 4   F 5   D 6

12. They enjoyed the fireworks while the american flag waved overhead and the band played the star spangled banner.

    A 4   K 5   L 6

Objective: Identify the need for capital letters in proper nouns: names, places, things, months, days, and holidays; practice editing skills.

15

Space Savers

Find the word or words that stand for the initials and abbreviations.

213 Pine **1** St.
Galesburg, Illinois 60401
2 Mar. 17, 2000

Dear **3** Dr. Dolan,

My father, **4** D. William, **5** Sr., and I would like to meet with you. Would it be possible for us to see you **6** Mon., March 28? We would like to visit with you at 3 **7** P.M., if possible.

8 Ms. Douglas will not be able to accompany us, but my father's assistant, **9** Mr. Kyle, will attend. Please plan for three visitors.

I will call you tomorrow at 9 **10** A.M. to confirm the date and time of our meeting. In the meantime, please send me the directions to your new office on Grand **11** Ave.

Thank you for your time and consideration. I look forward to seeing you on Monday.

Sincerely,

Douglas William, **12** Jr.

Answer Box

A	B	C	D	E	F
Senior	Avenue	Junior	a title for a woman	post meridiem	ante meridiem
G	**H**	**I**	**J**	**K**	**L**
Doctor	a title for a man	Monday	March	Douglas	Street

Objective: Identify whole words represented by abbreviations and initials; practice usage skills.

Peter Piper's Pickles

Consider This

Rules for Forming Possessive Nouns		
Type of Noun	**Add**	**Examples**
singular noun	' before the *s*	horse horse's
plural noun ending in *s*	' after the *s*	trees trees'
plural noun not ending in *s*	' before the *s*	children children's

Read each tongue twister. Choose the correct possessive form for each noun.

1 Betty bought a bit of butter.
B Betty's butter   H Bettys' butter

2 Seven silly sheep slept in a shack.
C sheeps' shack   J sheep's shack

3 Three tree toads tied together trotted to their tree.
E toads' tree   K toad's tree

4 A black-spotted haddock had big black spots.
J haddocks' spots   A haddock's spots

5 Eight apes ate eighty-eight apples.
I apes's apples   L apes' apples

6 A spiral-shelled sea snail shuffled in its sea shell.
D snails' shell   I snail's shell

7 Sister Sarah shined her silver shoes for Sunday.
H Sarah's shoes   G Sarahs' shoes

8 Two terrified tomcats were trapped in the tops of their tall trees.
A tomcat's trees   D tomcats' trees

9 Seven shy sailors salted their salmons standing shoulder to shoulder.
F sailors' salmons   E sailors's salmons

10 A tutor who tooted a flute tried to teach two tooters to toot.
G tutor's tooters   B tutors' tooters

11 How much wood would a woodchuck chuck, if a woodchuck could chuck wood?
K woodchuck's wood   F woodchucks's wood

12 Pop keeps a lollipop shop and the lollipop shop keeps Pop.
L Pops' shop   C Pop's shop

Objective: Identify the correct form of singular and plural possessive nouns; practice usage skills.

17

Olympic Action

> Remember, choosing the right verb will make the image more vivid.

Consider This

An **action verb** is a word or words that tell what the subject is doing or has done.

Jesse Owens ran track in the 1936 Summer Olympic Games.
↑
action verb

Read the two short articles about Olympic stars. Find the best action verb for each numbered space.

Mildred "Babe" Didrikson

Babe Didrikson **1** ▢ everyone at the Olympic tryouts in Evanston, Illinois, where she **2** ▢ three events. She **3** ▢ the javelin farther than any of her competitors; she **4** ▢ over the hurdles faster than all the others; and she **5** ▢ over the tallest high bar.

Two weeks later, Babe **6** ▢ two gold medals and one silver medal around her neck at the closing ceremonies in the 1932 Olympic games. She **7** ▢ onto the platform and received congratulations from the Olympic judges.

Greg Louganis

Unfortunately, Greg Louganis **8** ▢ his head on the springboard during a dive. He **9** ▢ he was a true champion when he continued to compete in the 1988 Summer Olympics in Seoul, South Korea. He **10** ▢ his way to two gold medals. He **11** ▢ his 1984 Olympic achievements where he had won gold in both the springboard and the platform diving events. Many people **12** ▢ his courage to continue diving after his injury on the springboard.

Answer Box

A	B	C	D	E	F
surprised	leaped	threw	proved	won	wore
G	**H**	**I**	**J**	**K**	**L**
dove	stepped	soared	matched	struck	admired

Objective: Identify action verbs, using context; practice grammar skills.

Verbs That Link

Consider This

A verb can show action, but it can also show a state of being. A **linking verb** connects the subject with a word or words in the predicate that rename or describe the subject. The most common linking verbs are a form of the verb *be*: *am, is, are, was, were,* and *been.* Other linking verbs include *seem, feel, look,* and *taste.*

> We are lost in this strange town.
> ↑
> linking verb

Find the word that is linked to the subject by the linking verb.

1. John Chapman was crazy about apples.
      A crazy   B apples   C was

2. The pioneers were hungry after a day on the trail to the West.
      C hungry   A were   K after

3. The trees' blossoms smelled heavenly in the spring.
      D spring   F heavenly   A smelled

4. An apple was perfect for a snack.
      I was   L snack   B perfect

5. In the fall, apples are bountiful in orchards.
      E are   H fall   L bountiful

6. John seemed content to roam the country planting apple trees everywhere he went.
      L seemed   D content   G trees

7. To him, apples tasted sweet as sugar.
      K sugar   C tasted   H sweet

8. John felt sorry for the hungry westward-bound travelers.
      B felt   I sorry   D hungry

9. He looked happy walking along in his bare feet.
      J bare   E happy   I looked

10. People were grateful to John Chapman, whom they nicknamed "Johnny Appleseed."
       G grateful   J to   F are

11. I am a lover of folklore and legends.
       H am   K lover   E folklore

12. Johnny Appleseed is a wonderful legendary character.
       F is   G legend   J character

Objective: Identify the word in the predicate that is connected to the subject by a linking verb, using context.

19

Do You Need Help?

Consider This

The **main verb** is the most important verb in the predicate. Sometimes a **helping verb** is used with the main verb to show when the action happened or when it will happen.

When using the helping verbs *am*, *is*, *are*, *was*, or *were*, the main verb often ends in *-ing*.

We <u>are</u> play<u>ing</u>.   He <u>was</u> runn<u>ing</u> outside.

When using the helping verbs *have*, *has*, or *had*, the main verb often ends in *-ed*.

They <u>have</u> finish<u>ed</u>.   She <u>has</u> cook<u>ed</u> the dinner.

When the helping verb is *will*, the main verb does not change its form.

It <u>will</u> rain.   You <u>will</u> study this page.

Read each sentence. Find the *main verb*.

1 A monkey is running down the street.

2 The gray langur monkeys were sitting together.

3 A langur will eat a lot of leaves in one day.

4 Loggers have cleared the forests.

5 I am thinking about the monkeys' habitat.

6 This endangered species was named after the Indian monkey god, Hanuman.

Read each sentence. Find the *helping verb*.

7 Some langurs will eat flowers, seeds, and fruit.

8 I am sitting next to one of these sacred monkeys.

9 A female langur is running after her baby.

10 Perhaps she was thinking that he might fall from the tree.

11 Farmers have cleared away many of the langurs' trees to make farmland.

12 Silvered, golden, and purple-faced langurs were named for their colors.

Answer Box

A	B	C	D	E	F
named	sitting	was	will	eat	is
G	H	I	J	K	L
were	am	running	cleared	thinking	have

Objective: Identify main verbs and helping verbs, using context; practice grammar skills.

Fun with Puns

Consider This

The form of a verb shows when the action takes place. A verb in the **past tense** shows action that has already happened. A verb in the **future tense** shows action that will happen.

The class <u>shared</u> word games. **past tense**

The class <u>will share</u> puns. **future tense**

Sentences in the past tense sometimes have a helping verb. Sentences in the future tense always have a helping verb.

Choose *past* or *future* to describe the tense of each verb in color.

1	"I will play a new game," mumbled Peg.	L past	G future
2	"I will have too many jobs to do," Tom chortled.	D past	I future
3	Tom bellowed, "The fire will go out!"	G past	H future
4	"The puppies look like mongrels," Tom will mutter.	A past	K future
5	Tom claimed, "That gold will be mine!"	I past	A future
6	"She will sew it sloppily," Tom needled.	J past	B future
7	Tom shouted with alarm, "I slept late!"	E past	L future
8	"Six and four will make ten?" Tom asked tentatively.	F past	D future
9	Tom shouted sternly, "You will step to the back of the boat!"	H past	J future
10	"I will not be a pilot next year," Tom explained.	K past	F future
11	"We will boil some steamers," Tom clamored.	B past	C future
12	Tom spoke softly, "My bicycle wheel will melt."	C past	E future

Objective: Identify the past tense and the future tense of verbs; practice grammar skills.

21

Early Americans Protest

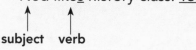

Consider This

Action verbs and helping verbs must agree with their subjects in number. Most verbs with a singular noun require *-s* or *-es* endings to make this agreement.

Ned likes history class. Tom and Giorgio like history class.

subject   verb   subject   verb

Choose the correct form of the verb in color.

1 Parliament (pass, passes) a new law.

2 The colonists (like, likes) tea.

3 They already (pay, pays) high taxes on tea.

4 The angry people (decide, decides) to stop buying tea because of the taxes.

5 Resistant American colonists (show, shows) their feelings.

6 One man (protest, protests) by throwing the boxes of tea off the ship into the harbor.

7 Another man (decide, decides) to join him, then another, and another.

8 The Boston Tea Party, as it was called, (show, shows) the British that the American colonists won't be easy to control.

9 Every colonist (pay, pays) a high price for this act of rebellion.

10 The members of Parliament (pass, passes) another law designed to keep colonial ships from leaving the harbor.

11 The British government (like, likes) the power it has over the American colonies.

12 The colonists (protest, protests) what they call the "Intolerable Acts" and discuss what to do at the first meeting of the Continental Congress.

Answer Box

A	B	C	D	E	F
passes	decide	show	likes	like	protests
G	**H**	**I**	**J**	**K**	**L**
decides	pass	pays	pay	protest	shows

Objective: Discriminate between correct and incorrect subject/verb agreement, using context; practice usage skills.

Tall Tales

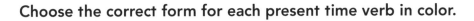

Consider This

Most verbs form the past tense by adding **-ed**. Verbs that do not follow this rule are called **irregular verbs**.

> Irregular verbs with the helping verbs <u>has</u>, <u>have</u>, or <u>had</u> often use the endings <u>n</u> or <u>en</u>.

Present	Past	Helping Verb + Past Participle
do	did	(has, have, or had) done
go	went	(has, have, or had) gone
grow	grew	(has, have, or had) grown
write	wrote	(has, have, or had) written

Choose the correct form for each present time verb in color.

American folklore has **1** give our culture many colorful tall tales. Here are some tall tales about Paul Bunyan. Paul Bunyan had **2** fall down as a child and flattened all the trees in his neighborhood. Paul's cooks **3** eat their way out of a popcorn blizzard. His loggers once had **4** eat an entire lake of pea soup. Paul's pet, Babe the Blue Ox, **5** run across the soft spring ground and his hoof prints created all the lakes in Wisconsin and Minnesota.

In another folktale, Pecos Bill had **6** ride his horse, Widowmaker, for many years, but one time he **7** ride a cyclone instead. Widowmaker could **8** run even faster than the cyclone.

Davy Crockett **9** come from Tennessee. He once **10** give a bear a hug that was too close for comfort!

John Henry had **11** come to work for the railroad on the Big Bend Tunnel. Huge rocks **12** fall beneath his hammer as he raced against the steam drill and won!

Answer Box

A	B	C	D	E	F
gave	rode	ate	came	run	fell

G	H	I	J	K	L
eaten	given	ran	come	ridden	fallen

Objective: Discriminate between past tense and past participle forms of irregular verbs; practice grammar skills.

Spoonerisms

> A spoonerism is the funny "mixing up" of the first syllables of words or initial sounds—<u>F</u>ave <u>H</u>un with this page!

Consider This

Past Tense and Past Participle Forms of Irregular Verbs

Some irregular verbs have the same form for the past participle as for the past tense.

| find | <u>found</u> | has <u>found</u> |

Some irregular verbs add *-n* to the past tense to form the past participle.

| break | broke | has broke<u>n</u> |

Some irregular verbs change one vowel each in the past tense and the past participle.

| dr<u>i</u>nk | dr<u>a</u>nk | has dr<u>u</u>nk |

Read each spoonerism. Decide if the verb in color is the *past tense* or the *past participle*.

1. You have broken my bater wottle!

2. The weather reporter spoke about show snowers.

3. I thought this was a tapter chest.

4. She caught a hish with a fook.

5. The song you sang bings a rell.

6. They had swum in a lake in Yew Nork.

7. He has spoken a lack of pies.

8. The polor crinter next to my computer just broke.

9. You have caught us stormbraining ideas for the party.

10. Mom has thought about putting bamburger huns on the shopping list.

11. I once swam in a pool of shilkmakes.

12. She has sung a lullabye for the children during teepy slime.

E	past tense	F	past participle
H	past tense	B	past participle
I	past tense	K	past participle
K	past tense	D	past participle
D	past tense	C	past participle
J	past tense	A	past participle
G	past tense	E	past participle
B	past tense	I	past participle
L	past tense	J	past participle
F	past tense	L	past participle
C	past tense	H	past participle
A	past tense	G	past participle

Objective: Identify past tense and past participle forms of irregular verbs; practice grammar skills.

Brainy Objects

Read each sentence and look for the verb.
Then find its *direct object*.

The direct object will answer the questions <u>whom</u> or <u>what</u> about the verb's action.

1. The human brain contains 100 billion neurons.

2. Bundles of neurons are called nerves.

3. These nerve cells form a web through which signals travel.

4. The brain controls everything in your entire body.

5. Each part of the brain governs a different job.

6. Messages reach the control center in your brain instantly.

7. Your brain stores information for your whole life.

8. Scientists study brain signals in laboratories.

9. A machine creates images that map active areas.

10. The images help scientists map brain activity.

11. Researchers can read a map of the different areas that work together on a job.

12. Use your brain by wearing a helmet when bicycle riding.

Answer Box

A	B	C	D	E	F
everything	neurons	nerves	center	web	images
G	H	I	J	K	L
information	scientists	signals	brain	job	map

Objective: Identify the direct object in a sentence; practice grammar skills.

Let's Make Contractions!

Consider This

The **subject pronouns** *I*, *you*, *he*, *she*, *it*, *we*, and *they* can be combined with the **verbs** *am*, *is*, *are*, *has*, *have*, *had*, *will*, *shall*, and *would* to form contractions. The letter or letters that are omitted are replaced by an *apostrophe* (**'**).

it + is = it's   he + will = he'll

Find the pair of words each contraction represents.

1 you've

2 they'll

3 we're

4 we'd

5 you're

6 we'll

7 they're

8 she's

9 he's

10 we've

11 I'm

12 it's

Remember, the subject pronoun <u>you</u> can be either singular or plural.

No offense, Barrie, but I don't think you quite have the hang of contractions yet.

We'd

We've

We'll

Answer Box ·

A	B	C	D	E	F
we shall	they will	we would	you have	we are	he is
G	**H**	**I**	**J**	**K**	**L**
she is	it has	we have	they are	I am	you are

Objective: Identify contractions formed with subject pronouns and verbs.

Our Favorite Player!

Consider This

A **pronoun** takes the place of a noun or nouns.

<u>Singular</u>	<u>Plural</u>
I, me, my, mine	we, us, our, ours
you, your, yours	you, your, yours
he, him, his	they, them, their, theirs
she, her, hers	
it, its	

Find the pronoun to replace the noun or nouns in color.

1 The baseball collided with the bat.

2 The ball flew over the people into a nearby backyard.

3 The ball traveled 565 feet and was found by a boy.

4 Mickey Mantle hit that ball in 1953.

5 Mickey's father and grandfather taught him to play ball.

6 Mickey's mother watched her son start out as a catcher.

7 A talent scout signed Mickey to play with New York's team.

8 Later, he was voted the people's Most Valuable Player.

9 In 1969, the New York Yankees "retired" Mickey's uniform number.

10 My father and I love to go to the ballgame.

11 Mickey Mantle's team is my mother's favorite team.

12 This Hall of Fame player is a hero to my family.

Answer Box

A	B	C	D	E	F
We	its	her	They	their	us

G	H	I	J	K	L
It	He	him	his	them	She

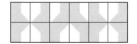

Objective: Identify singular and plural pronouns that can replace
nouns and noun phrases, using context.

27

He Climbed It

Match each sentence to a *simpler sentence* in which the subject noun has been replaced by a subject pronoun.

Remember, the subject part of a sentence names who or what the sentence is about.

1 In 1953, Edmund Hillary reached the top of Mt. Everest.

2 Mt. Everest is the highest mountain in the Himalayas.

3 The Himalayan Mountains form a range north of India in Nepal.

4 Native to the region, the Sherpas accompanied Hillary as guides.

5 People can run into many problems when climbing mountains.

6 Has a woman ever climbed Mt. Everest?

Identify the *subject pronoun* in each sentence.

7 You exercise when climbing and your muscles use oxygen faster.

8 At 29,000 feet above sea level, it is difficult to get oxygen into your blood.

9 I would be too afraid to climb it.

10 We would have to carry small tanks of oxygen up its slopes.

11 They would provide oxygen for us to breathe.

12 He was brave to climb to the top of it with his Sherpa guide.

Answer Box

A	B	C	D	E	F
You can have many problems.	They	They went along.	He reached the top.	He	it
G	**H**	**I**	**J**	**K**	**L**
They form a range.	I	You	We	Has she climbed Mt. Everest?	It is the highest mountain.

Objective: Identify subject pronouns; practice grammar skills.

I Object!

Pronouns can replace nouns as **direct objects** in the predicate.

Singular Object Pronouns: me, you, him, her, it

Plural Object Pronouns: us, you, them

Read the letter. Find the correct *subject* or *object pronoun* to replace the words in color.

A direct object **follows** an action verb.

Dear Margaret,

Dad and I are having a great time in Australia. We have seen many strange animals, including possums. **1** Possums live in trees. **2** A mother possum carries her babies in a pouch like other marsupials do. I think you would like **3** possums.

4 A brushtail possum is Australia's largest possum, but we have not seen one yet. **5** Dad and I saw a pygmy possum. The pygmy possum frightened **6** Dad and me because it looked like a rat.

7 Dad also discovered a marsupial mouse that was similar in size to the pygmy possum. Dad snuck up on a female sugar glider and frightened **8** the sugar glider. The sugar glider jumped from a branch right above **9** Dad. I wish **10** Margaret could have been there. It was so funny!

Maybe you can join **11** Laura next time. **12** Laura sure hope so!

Love,

Laura

Answer Box

A	B	C	D	E	F
us	She	you	He	them	him
G	H	I	J	K	L
her	I	It	They	me	We

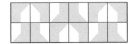

Objective: Discriminate between subject pronouns and object pronouns, using context; practice grammar skills.

29

Her Messy Meeting

Consider This

Possessive pronouns show ownership just as possessive nouns do, but possessive pronouns do not take an apostrophe.

<u>Arthur's</u> amazing animals. <u>His</u> amazing animals.

Singular Possessive Pronouns: my, mine, your, yours, his, her, hers, its

Plural Possessive Pronouns: our, ours, their, theirs

Find a possessive pronoun to take the place of the words in color.

1. The mother belonging to me had the library league over for lunch.

2. Unfortunately, my guinea pig pranced on Mr. Peterson's pecan pie.

3. Then, my cat climbed on the kitchen counter and knocked over Mrs. Carter's coffee cup.

4. Mrs. Francis found my supply of the frog's favorite flies and fainted.

5. The dog who dragged the tablecloth across the floor is my family's.

6. Mrs. Snickel was scared by my sister and brother's slimy snake.

7. The lizard that leaped into Lily Longly's lap is also my brother and sister's.

8. My family's fishbowl fell over, and the fantails went flipping and flopping across the floor.

9. The principal knocked on the door and said to me, "The mother that belongs to you called."

10. The hamsters had hidden in the old handbag that Mrs. Huckleberry thought was Mrs. Huckleberry's.

11. The principal asked me, "Are all of these animals ones that belong to you?"

12. "Yes, the majority of them are, so the mess is definitely one that belongs to me," I mumbled.

Answer Box

A	B	C	D	E	F
ours	yours	My mother	its	mine	Our

G	H	I	J	K	L
Your mother	her	hers	theirs	his	their

Objective: Identify possessive pronouns, using context; practice grammar and usage skills.

Look at Yourself!

Consider This

Reflective (or reflexive) **pronouns** are personal pronouns with the endings *-self* or *-selves*. They reflect the action of the verb back on the subject. They must agree with the subject in number and gender.

Kathy hurt herself.

singular noun   verb   singular pronoun

The boys hurt themselves.

plural noun   verb   plural pronoun

Use the clues about reflections to find the correct pronoun in the puzzle to take the place of the words in color.

Across

- **3** A bird sees its body in the mirror.
- **6** A girl sees her own face in the mirror.
- **7** I see my own face in the mirror.
- **8** We see our faces in the mirror.
- **10** You and your friends see each other in the mirror.
- **12** You see your own face in the mirror.

Down

- **1** Your friends see their faces in the mirror.
- **2** My friend and I see our faces in the mirror.
- **4** A boy sees his own face in the mirror.
- **5** I see my friends' faces in the mirror.
- **9** I see your face in the mirror.
- **11** The mirror reflects you and me.

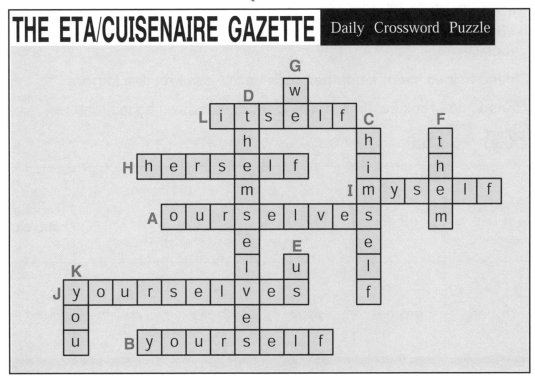

THE ETA/CUISENAIRE GAZETTE   Daily Crossword Puzzle

Objective: Identify reflective pronouns, subject pronouns, and object pronouns; practice grammar and usage skills.

Pronouns and Antecedents

Consider This

The **antecedent** is the noun or pronoun to which a pronoun refers. A pronoun must agree with its antecedent in number and gender.

John brought his mother the dish she wanted to wash.

antecedent pronoun antecedent pronoun

> The antecedent usually appears before the pronoun.

Find the correct antecedent for each pronoun in color.

1. I love the library because I think the books in it are exciting to read.
2. A good storybook can make you laugh, or it might make you cry.
3. I think reading exciting stories beats watching them on TV.
4. My favorite book belongs to my sister; it's her favorite too.
5. My brother loves comic books, but he sometimes reads fiction.
6. My brother and sister bring their books to the library.
7. My cousins own *Tom Sawyer*, and they also own *Moby Dick*.
8. My cousin works in the library, and she loves her job.
9. When I won the prize in the "Author's Contest," I was surprised to hear what it was; my cousin told me the news.
10. I could choose three books from the bookstore, and I couldn't wait to choose them.
11. My friend helped me pick out the books because she reads a lot too.
12. My friend and I took our time looking for books that we hadn't read yet.

Answer Box

A	B	C	D	E	F
prize	stories	books	cousins	storybook	brother and sister

G	H	I	J	K	L
friend	brother	sister	library	cousin	friend and I

Objective: Identify the antecedents of pronouns, using context; practice grammar and usage skills.